DO IT YOURSELF

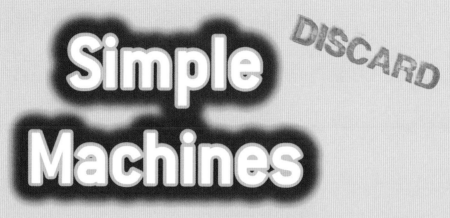

Simple Machines

Forces in Action

Buffy Silverman

Heinemann Library
Chicago, Illinois

© 2009 Heinemann Library
an imprint of Capstone Global Library, LLC
Chicago, Illinois

Customer Service 888-454-2279
Visit our website at www.heinemannraintree.com

Editorial: Louise Galpine and Rachel Howells
Design: Richard Parker and Tinstar Design Ltd
Original illustrations © Capstone Global Library Ltd
Illustrations: Oxford Designers and Illustrators
Picture research: Hannah Taylor and Fiona Orbell
Production: Alison Parsons

Originated by Dot Gradations Ltd.
Printed and bound in China by Leo Paper Products Ltd.

13 12 11 10 09
10 9 8 7 6 5 4 3 2 1

Library of Congress Cataloging-in-Publication Data
Silverman, Buffy.
  Simple machines : forces in action / Buffy Silverman.
     p. cm. -- (Do it yourself)
  Includes bibliographical references and index.
  ISBN 978-1-4329-2310-5 (hc) -- ISBN 978-1-4329-2317-4 (pb)
  1. Simple machines--Juvenile literature. I. Title.
  TJ147.S55 2009
  621.8--dc22
                            2008034936

Acknowledgments
The author and publishers are grateful to the following for permission to reproduce copyright material: © Alamy pp. 6 (Kim Karpeles), 23 (David Russell), **29 top** (Picture Contract), **29 bottom** (Wesley Hitt), 35 (Pixoi Ltd.), 37 (Nick Gregory), 39 (f1 online); © Blend Images/ Photolibrary p. 27; © Corbis pp. 4 (Construction Photography), 5 (Jose Fuste Raga), 12 (David Frazier), 13 (image100), 15 (pixland), 36 (Richard Hamilton Smith), 41 (Roger Wood), 43 (Randy Faris); © Dorling Kindersley p. 42 (Philip Gatward); © Getty pp. 17 (Stockbyte); © istock pp. 19 (Steven Robertson), 28 (James Knopf), 31; © Masterfile p. 25 (Kevin Dodge); © Photolibrary p. 21 (Odilon Dimier); © Tudor Photography p. 24 (Capstone Global Library Ltd.).

Cover photograph of gears, reproduced with permission of © Paul Eekhoff (Masterfile).

The publishers would like to thank Harold Pratt for his assistance in the preparation of this book.

Every effort has been made to contact copyright holders of any material reproduced in this book. Any omissions will be rectified in subsequent printings if notice is given to the publishers.

Disclaimer
All the Internet addresses (URLs) given in this book were valid at the time of going to press. However, due to the dynamic nature of the Internet, some addresses may have changed, or sites may have changed or ceased to exist since publication. While the author and publishers regret any inconvenience this may cause readers, no responsibility for any such changes can be accepted by either the author or the publishers. It is recommended that adults supervise children on the Internet

Contents

Any words appearing in the text in bold, **like this**, are explained in the glossary.

Timeless Machines

Powerful **machines** fill a construction site. Bulldozers move the earth, loaders carry gravel from one place to another, and cranes hoist heavy beams off the ground. A noisy **jackhammer** drills into the rocky ground. Construction workers rely on machines to build towering **skyscrapers** that soar to the sky. These machines use **electricity**, gasoline, or some other form of power.

Long ago, people did not have huge machines with engines and motors to help them lift and carry heavy **loads**. But they did have machines that helped them do **work**. People have been using machines for thousands of years.

Machines help people lift, carry, and dig at a construction site.

Building the pyramids

Ancient Egyptians built the pyramids out of huge stone blocks. They had to cut, carry, and lift massive blocks. Each block had to be placed in the right position. They could not do this without the help of machines. Workers used **levers** to help pick up the blocks and put them in the right spot. **Rollers** moved blocks from one place to another. As the pyramids grew taller, workers built **ramps** to move blocks up to a higher level.

Thousands of years ago, people used simple machines to build the pyramids.

Levers, rollers, and ramps are **simple machines** that help people do work. A machine is any device that allows work to be done with less **effort**. Effort is a **force** acting on an object that moves the object. The force might be pushing, pulling, or lifting. At the beach you use a shovel to help you lift and carry sand when you build a castle. The shovel is a simple machine that helps you do work.

Simple machines make moving something easier. This book explores the six types of simple machine: **inclined planes**, **wedges**, **screws**, levers, **wheels and axles**, and **pulleys**.

About the experiments

Carrying out the experiments in this book will help you to understand simple machines. The experiments use everyday materials and tools. Always read through the instructions before you start, and take your time. You will need an adult to help with some of the experiments.

Inclined Plane

Suppose you are building a wall from large rocks. You must lift heavy rocks into a wagon to bring them to the building site. The rocks are too heavy to lift, so you use a **ramp** to roll them into the wagon. When you push rocks up a ramp, you are using an **inclined plane** to help you do **work**. An inclined plane is a **simple machine**; it is a slanted surface used to raise or lower objects.

Furniture movers use an inclined plane to lift heavy **loads** onto a truck.

Historic planes

About 2,600 years ago, the ancient Greeks built a 6-km (3.7-mile) inclined plane to move boats overland. Instead of having to sail around a dangerous peninsula, boats were pulled along a track paved with limestone. The track was called the *Diolkos*, meaning "portage across."

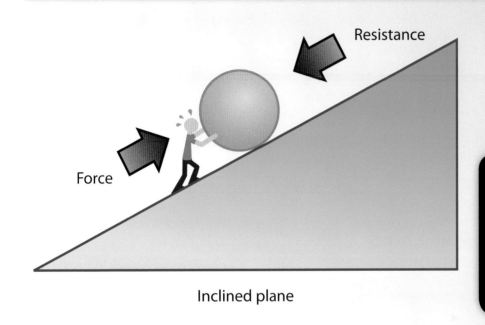

Resistance

Force

Inclined plane

An inclined plane adds distance to the work that must be done, but reduces the effort.

Distance versus effort

Why can you lift the rock into the wagon using the ramp, but not without it? It takes a certain amount of **effort** to lift a rock. The same amount of effort is required with a ramp, but an inclined plane changes the way you do the work. Instead of lifting the rock straight up, you push it along the ramp, over a longer distance. The extra distance means you do not have to use as much effort or **force**. If the distance along which you push a rock is twice as long, it takes half the force to do the same work and move the rock to the same height. There is a trade-off between the amount of effort required and the distance.

Imagine that you have a choice of two trails to climb to the top of a mountain. One route is short and steep, and the other trail is long and gentle. It will take the same amount of effort to reach the top no matter which trail you choose. But the steep trail requires more effort and less distance than the gentle trail. Which inclined plane will you climb?

Using an inclined plane

For this activity you will need:

* A table
* Two books, each about 5 cm (2 in.) thick
* A paper clip
* Scissors

1 Stack the books on the table.

2 Cut the rubber band, making one long piece.

3 Tie the paper clip to one end of the band.

4 Hang the rubber band from the top of the ruler, so the bottom of the paper clip reaches to 9 cm (3.5 in.) on the ruler.

* A ruler
* Sticky tape
* A rubber band
* A sandwich bag with twist tie
* A handful of gravel
* A piece of string, 30 cm (12 in.) long
* A smooth board, about 30 cm x 60 cm (1 ft. x 2 ft.)
* Paper and a pencil.

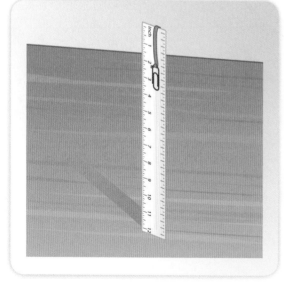

5 The other end of the rubber band hangs over the back of the ruler. Tape it to the back of the ruler.

6 Place gravel in the plastic bag, and fasten it closed with the twist tie.

7 Tie one end of the string around the bag and the other end to the paper clip.

8 Place the bag next to the books on the table. Hold the ruler and lift straight up until the bottom of the bag is at the level of the books. Observe where the paper clip stretches to, and record the number on the ruler at the tip of the paper clip.

9 Place the board on top of the books, making a ramp.

10 Holding the ruler, pull the bag to the top of the books. Observe where the paper clip reaches and record the number on the ruler corresponding to the tip of the paper clip.

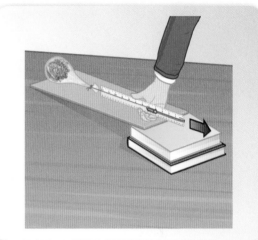

How does it work?

The amount that the rubber band stretched shows the effort needed to lift the gravel. Did it take more effort to lift the bag straight up, or to slide it up the ramp? You probably recorded a larger number when you lifted straight up. That means that it required more effort to lift the load up to the height of the books.

When you pulled the bag up the inclined plane, you pulled it farther but with less effort. Using an inclined plane makes it easier to lift a load by increasing the distance the load travels.

Penny power

For this activity you will need:
* Two books, each about 5 cm (2 in.) thick
* A smooth board, about 30 cm x 60 cm (1 ft. x 2 ft.)
* Plastic cup
* A piece of string, 1.5 meters (5 ft.) long
* Pennies
* Paper and a pencil
* A plastic container
* A hole puncher

1 Stack the two books near the edge of a table. Prop one end of the board on the books to make an inclined plane.

5 Drape the string over the end of the board, with the cup hanging down.

2 Punch two holes on opposite sides of the top of the cup. Thread one end of the string through the holes and tie it.

3 Tie the other end of the string under the lip of the plastic container.

4 Put the container on the ramp.

6 Place pennies in the cup, one at a time. Count and record the number of pennies needed to raise the container to the top of the board.

 7 Remove one book from under the end of the board.

 8 How many pennies do you think you will now need to lift the container to the top of this lower ramp? Record your estimate.

9 Repeat the experiment and count the number of pennies needed to lift the container to the top of the lower ramp.

How does it work?

You probably found that you needed fewer pennies to lift the container to a lower height. The distance traveled was the same because the length of the board was the same. But the height climbed was less, so it took less effort to do the work.

What would happen if you put a small toy inside the plastic container? Set up the ramp again, with two books underneath. Do you need more or fewer pennies to raise the container? When you add weight to the load in the container, it takes more effort to reach the top of the ramp.

We use many kinds of inclined planes to make it easier to lift heavy loads. Cars drive up ramps to reach highways. We climb stairs, an inclined plane, to reach the top of buildings. You ride your bicycle up a long, twisting road instead of a steep slope to make your climb easier.

Wedge

The **wedge** is a **simple machine** that is used to push things apart. It is made of two **inclined planes**, joined back-to-back. A wedge is wide at one end and thin at the other. An axe and the tip of a nail are examples of wedges.

When we use an inclined plane to do **work**, the inclined plane does not move. The object being lifted or lowered moves along the inclined plane. A wheelchair travels up a **ramp**, and the wheelchair moves, but the ramp stays still. The inclined plane makes the **effort** easier by using a longer distance to lessen the amount of effort needed to lift a **load**.

A wedge is a moving inclined plane. It uses **force** to come between two things. An axe is swung into a log. When the axe hits the log, the force is pushed from above to the sides and splits the log apart. A wedge changes the direction of the force that is applied to something.

A wedge is hammered into a log, and the log splits apart.

Skinny wedges

The sharper the point or narrower the edge of a wedge, the less effort it takes to push an object apart. You can push a thin wedge a longer distance than a thick wedge, but with less effort. The blade of a knife is a wedge with a thin, sharp edge. When you slice an apple with a sharp knife it does not take much effort. The force that you apply to the knife handle moves the thin blade, which pushes apart the apple.

You have a wedge inside you—your teeth! You can split an apple by using your jaw muscles to push your teeth into it. Your front teeth move up and down, and the apple splits apart.

A doorstop is a wedge used to hold things. By pushing the thin edge of the wedge underneath the door, the door is raised. The door pushes the wedge down against the floor, holding it in place.

When you chew an apple, your teeth act as wedges that split the apple apart.

Wedges at work

For this activity you will need:

* Two wooden building blocks (rectangular shaped)
* One skinny wedge-shaped block (a ramp or roof piece from a building block set)
* One fat wedge-shaped block (as above)
* A ruler
* Paper and a pencil.

1 Line up the two blocks so they are side by side. The narrow ends of the blocks should be touching.

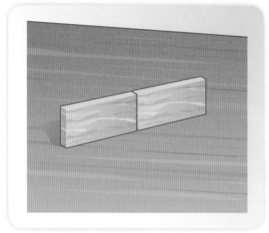

3 With the ruler, measure the distance between the ends of the blocks after being separated by the wedge. Record the distance between the blocks.

2 Push the skinny wedge between the blocks, from above.

4 Move the blocks together again. Now push the fat wedge between them, from above.

5 Measure the distance between the ends of the blocks, and record it.

How does it work?

What happened when a wedge was pushed between the blocks? You pushed from above, exerting a downward force on the blocks. Because of the shape of the wedge, the blocks moved to the sides. The wedge changed the direction of the force from downward to sideways.

The thickness of a wedge changes the amount of work that can be done with the wedge. How far apart did the blocks move with the thick and thin wedges? You pushed the wedge down the same distance, from the top of the blocks to the bottom of the blocks. But the thick wedge made the blocks slide farther apart than the thin wedge. A thick wedge can move something a farther distance, but it requires more effort. Because the blocks were easy to separate, you probably could not feel the difference in the effort needed to move them apart with the thick and thin wedges.

Cutting with wedges

Many cutting tools use wedges to do work. The blades of a scissors form two wedges that move in opposite directions. They cut material where they meet. A can opener has a wedge-shaped cutting wheel that pushes into a can's lid. An electric shaver has many wedge-shaped blades that slice through hair. A plow is a wedge-shaped tool that cuts the top layer of soil, then lifts and turns it over.

Each tooth of a saw is a wedge that cuts through wood.

1 Measure and record the length of each nail.

2 Ask an adult to strike the thin nail 10 times with the hammer, hammering it into the block of wood. They should wear safety goggles.

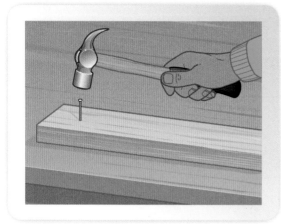

Wedge power

For this activity you will need:

* A block of scrap wood (soft wood such as pine, if available), about 5 cm (2 in.) thick
* A hammer
* A thin nail
* A nail of medium thickness
* A thick nail
* A ruler
* Paper and a pencil
* Safety goggles.

⚠ **Warning**: Adult help will be needed for this experiment.

3 Measure how much of the nail sticks out from the block of wood. To calculate how far the nail was driven into the wood, subtract the length sticking out of the wood from the total length of the nail. Record this length.

4 Ask an adult to strike the medium nail 10 times with the hammer, into the block of wood.

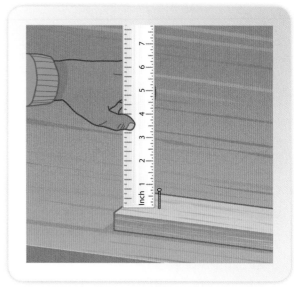

5 Measure how much of the medium nail sticks out from the block of wood. Calculate and record how far the nail was driven into the wood.

6 Ask an adult to strike the thick nail 10 times with the hammer, into the block of wood.

7 Measure how much the thick nail sticks out from the block of wood. Calculate and record how far the nail was driven into the wood.

How does it work?

Which of the nails was easiest to hammer into the wood? Which nail went farthest into the wood?

You probably found that it was easier to hammer a thin nail into the wood than a thick nail. The thin nail is easier to hammer because the point of the nail (the wedge) is thinner. It takes less effort to push the thin wedge into the wood because it makes a smaller hole. The thicker nail makes a wider opening in the wood. It requires more effort to push aside more wood fibers to make the larger hole.

The tip of a nail is a wedge that pushes apart wood, driving the nail into the wood. Nails can be used to fasten two pieces of wood together.

Screw

Look closely at a **screw** and you will find another **simple machine**. A screw is made of an **inclined plane** wrapped around a cylinder. A screw has three parts: the head, shaft, and tip. Examine the shaft of a screw and you see **threads** wound around it. If you could straighten these threads, they would form an inclined plane.

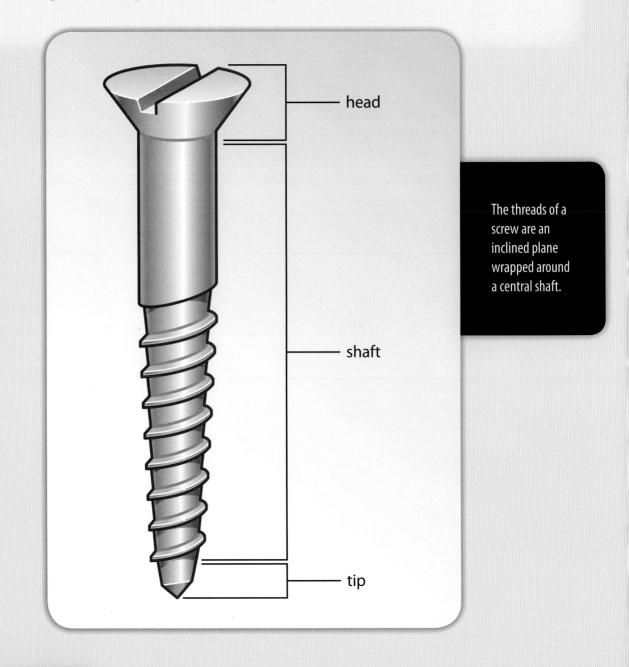

head

shaft

tip

The threads of a screw are an inclined plane wrapped around a central shaft.

Lessening the effort

An inclined plane lessens the **effort** needed to lift or lower something by increasing the distance over which the **work** is done. A screw allows work to be done in the same way—with less effort. The threads of a screw turn around and around as they cut into wood or other materials. Less effort is needed to cut into the wood because of the increased distance that the threads travel.

You can demonstrate how turning a screw a long distance lessens the effort needed to do work. Examine the lid of a peanut butter jar or other type of jar with a screw-on cap. The inside of the lid is a screw with a thread. The threads turn and grip the jar as you open and close it. Place the lid on the jar, and turn it closed. Your hand moves around several times to screw the lid on as it travels a short distance up or down. You do not have to turn the lid with great **force**. Instead, you turn it a longer distance by moving your hand around and around.

A construction auger is a screw that drills holes deep into the ground.

Moving in circles

Like a **wedge**, a screw is designed to change the direction of force. Turn a screwdriver in a circle, and the threads of the screw cut down into a plank of wood. The circular motion of the screwdriver is changed into forward motion as the screw moves up or down. The blades of a fan are another type of screw that changes the direction of force. The blades turn around and around, pulling air in and pushing it out.

Making a screw

For this activity you will need:

* A pencil
* A sheet of paper (210 mm x 297 mm / 8.5 in. x 11 in.)
* A colored marker
* Scissors
* A ruler.

1 You can prove that a screw is an inclined plane by making a screw. Make a mark at 13 cm (5 in.) along the bottom of a sheet of paper. Draw a mark at 23 cm (9 in.) up the side of the paper. With a ruler, draw a line connecting the two marks. You will have drawn a right triangle, measuring 13 cm x 23 cm x 28.5 cm (5 in. x 9 in. x 10.3 in.).

2 Color the slanted edge of the inclined plane (the longest edge of the triangle) with the marker.

3 Cut the triangle from the paper, along the line. Notice that the triangle is the shape of a **ramp**, or inclined plane.

4 Position the shortest side (13 cm or 5 in.) of the triangle along the side of the pencil. Evenly wrap the paper around the pencil by rolling the pencil.

How does it work?

When you wrapped your inclined plane around the pencil, you made a screw. The long side of the inclined plane (the colored edge) was wound around the shaft of the screw. This colored edge represents the threads of a screw.

Screws that hold

The model that you made of a screw cannot hold material together, but that is the job of many screws. The threads of a wood screw push against wood, and hold pieces of wood firmly in place. The screw on a vise brings clamps together which hold an object tightly. A water faucet also has a screw inside. The screw moves a stopper to stop the flow of water or to let water flow out. The base of many light bulbs have screws that let them fit securely in a lamp. What other types of screws can you find in your home?

A screw with narrow threads is easier to turn than one with wider threads. Narrow threads are spaced closer together, so it takes more turns to tighten the screw, but less effort. These children are tightening the screws on their skateboard.

Steps to follow

For this activity you will need:

* An empty can (a tall can works best)
* Clear plastic tubing (about four times as long as the can is high)
* Masking tape
* A large bowl
* Water
* Food coloring.

1 You can make a screw that can lift water up from a bowl. Tape the clear plastic tubing to the top of the can.

2 Wind the tubing around the can, so it spirals like the threads of a screw.

3 Tape the tubing securely to the bottom of the can. Add one or two pieces of tape in the middle of the spiral, so the tubing stays securely on the can.

4 Add water to the bowl, filling it about halfway. Leave the bowl in the kitchen sink to avoid spills.

5 Carefully add three drops of food coloring to the water.

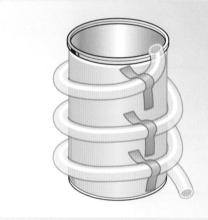

6 Tilting the can slightly, place the top end in the water. Turn the can until you see colored water in the tubing.

7 Carefully lift the can so it is above the water. Keeping the can tilted, continue to turn it. What happens to the water in the tube?

How does it work?

The screw that you made is a **machine** called an **Archimedes' screw**. Like all screws, it changes the direction of force. When you turned the screw with a circular movement, the water moved upward in the threads.

About 2,300 years ago, it is thought that a scientist named **Archimedes** invented a machine like this for lifting water. It was used to pump water from mines and ship holds and for **irrigation**. The Archimedes' screw had threads wound around a central shaft, inside a hollow pipe. When the screw is turned, it scoops up water and carries it up the pipe. Using an Archimedes' screw, a farmer could lift water from a stream or pond to an irrigation ditch. Archimedes' screws are still used for irrigation in many parts of the world. They are also used for lifting in other machines, such as combine harvesters.

Archimedes' screws are used as water pumps to irrigate land. They can be turned by people or by animals.

Lever

You buy a can of paint. The lid of the can fits tightly, so the paint does not leak out. You try to pull it off, but it does not budge. How will you loosen the lid? You might fit the blade of a screwdriver under the lid of the can. When you push down on the screwdriver handle, the lid pops up. You are using the screwdriver as a **lever**, a **simple machine** that does **work**.

A lever consists of a bar that moves up and down and tilts on a certain point. The point on which the bar tilts is called the **fulcrum**. You apply **force** to one part of a lever by pushing or pulling it. The force is called the **effort**, and the object moved by a lever is called the **load**.

To pry a tightly fitting lid off a can, you need a lever.

Effort and load

If you have ever played on a seesaw, you have been both the effort and the load on a lever. Imagine that you are trying to lift a person who is much heavier than you. You are the effort, trying to lift a heavy load. How will you do it? If the fulcrum is the same distance between both people on the seesaw, you will be stuck. But if the heavier person moves closer to the fulcrum and you move further from the fulcrum, you will be able to lift your load with less effort. Then it will be your turn to be the load that the other person lifts! As with an **inclined plane**, there is a trade-off between the amount of effort and the distance moved.

The word *lever* is from the French word meaning "to raise." More than 2,300 years ago, the scientist **Archimedes** understood how, with enough distance, a lever could raise a heavy object. He said, "Give me a lever long enough and a fulcrum on which to place it and I shall move the world."

With the help of a lever, children can lift a heavier person.

Steps to follow

1 Make a simple balance to find out how levers work. Fill the bottle with water, put the cap on tightly, and lay the bottle down flat. Tape the bottle down so it does not roll around. The water bottle will be the fulcrum on which your lever rests.

Make a dime balance

For this activity you will need:

* A small plastic water bottle
* A ruler
* Ten dimes
* Sticky tape.

2 Place a ruler over the water bottle. The ruler is the lever arm.

5 Stack five dimes on each side, and adjust them until they balance.

3 Try to make the ruler balance. To do so, you will have to place the mid-point of the ruler (15 cm or 6 in. mark) on the fulcrum.

6 Remove one dime from one side, and place it on the opposite side. Adjust the placement of the stacks so that six dimes will balance with four dimes.

4 Carefully place one dime on each end of the lever arm until the lever balances again. Place the dimes on the 3 cm (1 in.) and 27 cm (11 in.) marks.

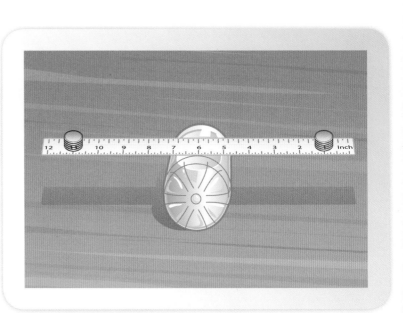

7 Predict where you will need to place the dimes to balance seven dimes and three dimes. Test and see if your prediction is correct.

8 Can you balance a stack of eight dimes and a stack of two? If you cannot balance them on your ruler, consider how you might change your balance. Find a longer lever arm, and see if your balance will work. With a longer lever arm, can you balance a stack of nine dimes with a single dime?

How does it work?

By adjusting the distance between the load and the fulcrum, you can balance a large stack of dimes with a small stack. The large stack of dimes pushes down with more force than the smaller one. A lever allows you to balance different forces by changing the distance from the fulcrum. By moving the effort farther from the fulcrum, less effort is needed and a smaller force can balance a larger one.

A balance is a type of lever that measures weight. The two sides are balanced by sliding weights closer to or farther from the fulcrum.

What kind of lever?

Levers are simple machines that allow effort to move something more easily by increasing the force applied to another object. Many tools that you use every day are levers. There are three different kinds of lever. The position of the fulcrum, effort, and load differs for each type. Search for each type of lever in your home.

First-class lever: In a first-class lever, the fulcrum is between the effort and the load. When force is applied, the effort moves in the opposite direction. Push down on a seesaw, and the person on the other side goes up. Boat oars and the claw of a hammer are first-class levers. Can you find others?

Pull down on the handle of this first-class lever to pry a nail from a board.

This second-class lever lets you lift a heavy load of dirt.

Second-class lever: In a second-class lever, the load is between the fulcrum and the effort. A wheelbarrow is a second-class lever. The fulcrum (the wheel) is at one end, the effort (your hands) at the other, and the load in the middle. You can raise a heavy load because it is closer to the fulcrum than the effort. The long handles of a wheelbarrow add the distance needed to lift loads with less effort. A nutcracker and a bottle opener are also second-class levers. What other second-class levers can you find?

Swing the handle of a third-class lever, and the ball soars away.

Third-class lever: In a third-class lever, the effort is between the fulcrum and the load. A fishing rod is a third-class lever. The fulcrum (the balancing hand) is at one end, the effort (the hand used to pull up the fish) is in the middle, and the load (the fish) is at the other end. When you catch a fish, the fish is lifted up farther than the distance your hand lifts on the rod. The distance it travels can be greater because it is farther from the fulcrum. A broom, shovel, tennis racquet, and hockey stick are all third-class levers. What others can you find?

Pulley

Imagine lifting a grand piano up a narrow flight of stairs. How could you make such a difficult job easier? You might tie a rope around the piano and use a **pulley** on a crane to hoist it up to a window, and then bring it inside. A pulley is a **simple machine** that lets you pull down to lift something up. A pulley consists of a wheel with a rope, belt, or chain wrapped around it. Pulling the rope down lifts the object attached to the pulley. With some pulleys, the direction of **force** is changed.

The simplest type of pulley is a single pulley. One wheel is fixed to a support, and a rope is attached to the **load** and looped over the wheel. When the rope is pulled down, the load moves up the same distance. A single pulley does not change the **effort** needed to lift a load, but it seems easier because you are pulling down instead of lifting up.

With this single pulley, you pull down on a rope and the load moves up the same distance.

Less effort is needed to lift a load with a double pulley, but the rope must be pulled a farther distance.

Easy lifting

Some pulleys reduce the effort needed for lifting. A double pulley has two wheels that are connected. One wheel is attached to the load, and the other wheel is fixed to a support. The rope passes over the top wheel, loops around the lower wheel, and back up to the top wheel. When the rope is pulled, the load moves only half the distance. Because the distance is decreased, the force is increased. A double pulley can lift twice as much weight with the same effort. By increasing the number of pulleys that are connected together, more and more weight can be lifted with the same effort.

A ski lift uses giant pulleys that help bring skiers up the mountain.

Powerful pulleys

Archimedes wanted to prove the power of a pulley to the king. He designed a complicated pulley system that moved a ship into the sea with just a few movements of his hand. The ship had needed many laborers to move it into position without pulleys.

Steps to follow

Make a pulley

For this activity you will need:
* Empty thread spools
* About 2.5 meters (8 feet) of string
* Four twist ties
* Scissors
* A pail with a handle
* Rocks.

1 Make a single, **fixed pulley**. Twist two twist ties together, to form one long tie.

2 Thread the long tie through the spool and twist it securely to a closet bar or other fixed point.

3 Place rocks inside the pail, so that it is heavy to lift.

6 Turn your single pulley into a double pulley. Untie the knot from the long string to the pail.

4 Loop the long string over the spool. Attach one end of the string to the handle of the pail.

5 Pull down on the other end to raise the load. Was the pail harder or easier to lift?

7

Twist the other two ties together. Thread this long tie through the second spool, and twist it securely to the handle of the pail. This forms a **moveable pulley** that moves with the load.

Pull on the free end of the long string to raise the load. Was the pail harder or easier to lift than with the single pulley?

Tie one end of the long string to the closet bar. Loop the long string under the lower pulley (attached to pail), and back up and over the top of the upper pulley.

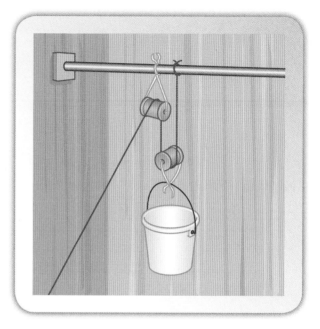

How does it work?

A single pulley does not change the effort required to lift a load. The distance you pull is the same as the distance that the pail travels. Since it is easier to pull than to lift an object, the pulley might have made lifting the pail easier.

Your heavy pail probably seemed lighter when you lifted it with a double pulley. A double pulley can lift more weight, but you must pull farther. The load travels half the distance that you pull the string. By increasing the distance that you pull, the effort needed to lift the load is decreased.

How could you make your pulley pull even more weight? Experiment with a four-pulley system using pairs of spools side by side.

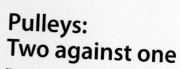

Pulleys: Two against one

For this activity you will need:

* Two friends
* Two brooms (or two poles about as thick as a broom handle)
* Rope (about 3 meters / 10 feet).

You can make a moveable pulley that will move your friends. Tie one end of the rope to one broom handle.

Ask your two friends to stand facing each other about 75 cm (2.5 ft.) apart. Have each person hold a broom handle in front, so that the brooms are about 60 cm (2 ft.) apart. The broom handles will be the wheels of your pulley.

Wrap the rope around the handles two more times. Now try to pull your friends while they pull the brooms away.

Wrap the rope around the broom handles two times.

Stand facing your friends, and hold on to the free end of the rope.

Try to pull your friends toward you while they pull the brooms away from each other.

How does it work?

Could you pull both your friends? Unless you are very strong, you probably were not able to pull them with the rope wrapped twice around the broom handles. The broom handles that you used were the pulleys that a rope wrapped around. When you wrapped the rope around the pulleys two more times, you decreased the effort needed to pull the load. By increasing the distance over which the force was applied, it took less effort to move the load. Now you could move both your friends!

A moveable pulley like the one you made with broom handles does not change the direction of the force. The load moved in the direction that you pulled.

Machines that use both fixed and moveable pulleys are called combined pulleys. A fixed pulley changes the direction of the force. One or more moveable pulleys multiply the amount of force acting on the load, so less effort is needed for lifting.

A crane has moveable pulleys with hooks that attach to the load that is being raised. It also has fixed pulleys attached to the crane arm.

Wheel and Axle

Walk along any city street and you see wheels on cars, trucks, buses, and bicycles. Wheels help people travel from place to place. Grip a doorknob or turn a faucet, and you are also using wheels that allow you to do **work** with less **effort**.

Most wheels are attached to an axle that goes through the wheel and moves along with it. A **wheel and axle** is a type of **simple machine**. A wheel and an axle turn together, so a **force** that is applied to one moves the other.

Big wheels help a heavy tractor move across a field.

Less distance, more force

A wheel and axle works in the same way as a **lever**. The center part of an axle is the **fulcrum** around which the wheel rotates. As it rotates, the outer edge of the wheel travels a greater distance than the axle in the center. The axle moves less distance and turns with greater force.

Try turning a **screw** with a screwdriver. You grip the screwdriver handle (the wheel), and the shaft in the center (the axle) turns the screw. The outside of the screwdriver moves a greater distance than the shaft, so the shaft turns with greater force. A wheel and axle can change a small force into a larger one.

A wheel and axle can also work to increase the distance that is traveled. A motor spins the axle of a fan, and the attached blades move farther, pushing air. When the axle of a Ferris wheel is turned, people riding in cars attached to the edge get an exciting ride.

Turning the handle of a screwdriver makes the shaft move with more force.

Easy rolling

When two objects rub against each other, they create **friction**. Friction is a force that slows objects down. If you pull a large box across the floor, the bottom drags against the floor, and friction slows the movement. Place the box on a cart, and only the wheels touch the ground. There is less friction, so it takes less effort to move the box.

Wheels at work

For this activity you will need:

* A ruler
* A rubber band
* A roller skate, a skateboard, a tricycle, or a wagon
* Paper and a pencil.

1 Attach the rubber band to the front of the roller skate or other wheeled object.

2 Measure and record the length of the attached rubber band.

3 Pull the skate by the rubber band, with its wheels on the ground. Measure and record the length of the rubber band as you pull.

4 Put the skate on its side and pull the skate again. Measure and record the length of the rubber band as you pull.

How does it work?

You probably found that the rubber band stretched farther when the skate was on its side. The rubber band stretched farther because it took more force to drag the skate without wheels. Wheels reduce the amount of force needed to move the skate by reducing friction. Instead of the entire surface of the skate rubbing against the ground, only the bottom of the wheels touched the ground.

Where do you use wheels?

Wheels and axles on bicycles, scooters, skateboards, wagons, and cars make it easier for us to move people and things. We also use many other types of wheel and axles for work and play. Look in your kitchen for wheels such as stove dials, rolling pins, and fans. Faucet handles, wrenches, and screwdrivers are wheels that increase force when they are turned. Gears are also wheels, with teeth meshed together to transmit force. Your kitchen clock and eggbeater might have gears. Take a close look at a CD spinning in a CD player and you will see a wheel and axle at work. What other wheels can you find?

Gears inside a clock move the clock hands.

Ancient wheels

The wheel is one of the world's oldest inventions. The first wheels were probably logs used as **rollers** under heavy **loads**. About 7,000 years ago, people in Mesopotamia used potter's wheels to shape clay pots. Carts with solid wooden wheels were used about 6,000 years ago. People also made water wheels that lifted water from streams to use for **irrigation**.

Steps to follow

Make a wheel and axle

For this activity you will need:

* One square piece of paper, 15 cm x 15 cm (6 in. x 6 in.)
* A pencil
* Scissors
* A ruler
* A hole puncher
* Thread
* A paper clip
* Sticky tape.

1 Draw two diagonal lines from one corner of the square paper to the opposite corner. The lines should cross in the center of the paper. Mark each line 2.5 cm (1 in.) from the center.

2 Cut along the lines from the corners, stopping at the marks.

3 Punch a hole in the upper left corner of each flap. With a pencil point, make a hole of the same size through the center (where the lines meet).

4 Curl up the corner holes, so they meet at the center hole. Push the straw through all five holes, and slide the pinwheel to the center of the straw.

5 Put a ring of tape around the straw, on each side of the pinwheel. The tape will keep the pinwheel in the center while still allowing it to spin.

6 Cut a piece of thread about 30 cm (12 in.) long. Tie the thread to one end of the straw, about 4 cm (1.5 in.) from the edge. Tape the thread loop securely to the straw, so it will not slide. Tie a paperclip to the other end of the thread.

7 Hold both ends of the straw loosely between your fingers. Blow on the pinwheel, allowing it to spin. What happens to the paperclip?

The blades of a windmill are fixed to an axle that turns with great force.

How does it work?

Notice how turning the pinwheel moves the axle (the straw), since both are attached. The spinning axle winds the thread, raising the paperclip. Since the wheel turns a greater distance than the axle, the force with which the axle turns is increased. It has enough force to raise the paper clip.

A windmill works in a similar way to your pinwheel. Wind turns the blades of a windmill, moving a vertical shaft with great force. Windmills were once used to grind grain and pump water. Modern wind turbines turn wind power into **electricity**.

Many Machines Make One

Simple machines help us do **work** by changing the size or direction of a **force**. Most **machines** are more complex than a simple machine. A machine that consists of two or more simple machines working together is called a **compound machine**.

Bike wheels

How many simple machines combine to make a bicycle go? The first simple machine you might notice on a bike is the **wheel and axle**. Only a small surface of a bicycle wheel touches the ground, reducing **friction**. Bicycle wheels look very different from the solid wooden wheels that moved carts thousands of years ago. Spokes make them strong but light. Each spoke is like a **lever** turning around the **fulcrum** at the center of a wheel.

How many wheels
are on this bicycle?

Look closely at a bike to find other wheels. Gears are wheels that have tiny teeth on them. The gears of a bike change the amount of force needed to pedal the bike with the distance turned. In a high gear, the chain moves to a smaller rear gear wheel and the rear wheel turns faster. The chain moves only a short distance to turn the wheel. It is harder to push the pedals, but the bike goes farther with each turn of the pedals. In a low gear, the chain moves to a larger rear gear wheel and the rear wheel turns more slowly. It takes less **effort** to push the pedals, but the bicycle travels a shorter distance. The teeth on the gears are another simple machine. They are **wedges** that mesh with the chain.

Bike levers

Can you find any levers on a bike? The arms that the pedals attach to are levers that turn a **pulley**. To stop a bike, you pull on brake levers. Brake levers attach to another set of levers by a cable. The second set of levers pull the rubber brakes against the wheels. The levers that you pull with your hand move a farther distance than the levers pulling the brakes, so the force is increased. So, what we think of as one machine, a bicycle, in fact contains many different types of simple machines.

Screws hold the parts of a bicycle together.

Glossary

Archimedes Greek mathematician and physicist who lived about 2,300 years ago and made many discoveries

Archimedes' screw ancient machine for lifting water, which is still used today. It consists of an inclined tube containing a broad-threaded screw.

compound machine machine made of two or more simple machines. A bicycle is a compound machine because it has levers, pulleys, and wheels.

effort force needed to use a simple machine

electricity form of energy that we use to operate many devices and machines

first-class lever lever with a fulcrum between the effort and load. A see-saw is a first-class lever.

fixed pulley single pulley that is attached to something not moveable

force physical quantity that denotes ability to push, pull, or twist

friction effort used when one object rubs against another. Friction slows down the movement of objects.

fulcrum point on which a lever balances. You can move the fulcrum to make an object easier to lift.

inclined plane simple machine with a slanted surface that is used to raise or lower objects. An inclined plane adds distance that an object must be lifted, but reduces the amount of effort needed to lift it.

irrigation supplying water to land, so that plants and crops can grow. The Archimedes' screw has been used to help irrigate land for more than 2,000 years.

jackhammer hand-held tool used to drill through rocks and break up pavement. It works by jabbing at the area with its bit.

lever simple machine that consists of a bar pivoting from a fulcrum. A lever allows you to lift a heavy load with less effort, but the distance moved is greater.

load object or weight that is moved by a simple machine. The heavier the object, the bigger the load.

machine mechanical or electrical device that helps people do work

moveable pulley pulley that moves with a load

pulley simple machine made of a wheel with a rope or chain wrapped around it. A pulley is used to lift objects.

ramp inclined surface along which an object is moved up or down. A ramp reduces the amount of force that is required, allowing the object to be moved more easily.

roller long tube that turns. The first rollers that were placed under heavy objects to move them were probably logs.

screw simple machine made of an inclined plane wrapped around a shaft. A bolt and a spiral staircase are types of screws.

second-class lever lever with a fulcrum at one end, effort at the other end, and a load in between. A wheelbarrow is a second-class lever.

simple machine machine with few or no moving parts that allows people to use less effort to move something. There are six types of simple machines: inclined plane, wedge, screw, lever, pulley, and wheel and axle.

skyscraper very tall building. The Taipei 101 in Taiwan is the world's tallest completed skyscraper. It is 501 meters (1,653 feet) tall!

third-class lever lever with a fulcrum at one end, a load at the other, and effort in between. A hockey stick is a third-class lever.

thread continuous ridge that spirals around a screw. Straightening these threads would form an inclined plane.

wedge simple machine made of two inclined planes joined back-to-back. An axe and knife are wedges.

wheel and axle simple machine with a large wheel connected to a central shaft that moves together. When a wheel is turned the axle moves a shorter distance, with more force.

work measure of energy used to move an object. Simple machines help people do everyday work.

Find Out More

Books

Auch, Allison. *Cool Tools*. (Minneapolis, Minn.: Compass Point Books, 2005)

Solway, Andrew. *Castle Under Siege! Simple Machines*. (Chicago: Raintree, 2005)

Thompson, Gare. *Lever, Screw, and Inclined Plane: The Power of Simple Machines*. (Washington, D.C.: National Geographic Children's Books, 2006)

Tocci, Salvatore. *Experiments with Simple Machines*. (Danbury, Conn: Children's Press, 2003)

Woods, Michael and Mary Woods. *Ancient Machines: From Wedges to Waterwheels*. (Minneapolis, Minn.: Twenty-First Century Books, 2000)

Websites

Edheads
www.edheads.org/activities/simple-machines
Explore the house and toolshed to find out more about simple machines.

Mikids
www.mikids.com/Smachines.htm
Learn about each of the six **simple machines** and do some simple machine activities

Rube Goldberg
www.rubegoldberg.com
Learn about Rube Goldberg's ingenious inventions.

Investigate and Report on Simple Machines
www.teacher.scholastic.com/dirtrep/simple
Dirtmeister helps you discover what simple machines are and where you can find them

The Franklin Institute
www.fi.edu/qa97/spotlight3
Great information about the six types of simple machine.

Places to visit

Museum of Science
1 Science Park
Boston, MA 02114
Tel: (617) 723-2500
www.mos.org

Investigate the push and pull of everyday life with playground equipment, bicycle parts, and more.

Museum of Science and Industry
57th Street and Lake Shore Drive
Chicago, IL 60637
Tel: (773) 684-1414
www.msichicago.org

Explore the energy and work behind simple machines in the Learning Lab.

Ontario Science Centre
770 Don Mills Road
Toronto, Ontario
Tel: (886) 696-1110
www.ontariosciencecentre.ca

Experiment with technology and explore simple machines.

Index